EMERGENCIES THAT COULD HAPPEN TO YOU, and HOW TO HANDLE THEM

By MARY LOU VANDENBURG • Illustrated by R.L. MARKHAM

Lerner Publications Company
Minneapolis, Minnesota

To Jamey, Laurie,
and Terry

LIBRARY OF CONGRESS CATALOGING IN PUBLICATION DATA

Vandenburg, Mary Lou.
  Help! Emergencies that could happen to you, and how to handle them.

  SUMMARY: Presents everyday emergencies involving fire, lightning, animal and insect bites, and swimming and skating accidents, and discusses common-sense solutions to these situations.

  1. Safety education—Juvenile literature. 2. Accidents—Juvenile literature. 3. First aid in illness and injury—Juvenile literature. [1. Safety education. 2. Accidents. 3. First aid] I. Markham, R. L. II. Title.

HV675.5.V35 1975   614.8'8   75-7007
ISBN 0-8225-0020-5

Cover design by Richard Gravender

Published simultaneously in Canada by J. M. Dent & Sons (Canada) Ltd., Don Mills, Ontario

Manufactured in the United States of America

International Standard Book Number: 0-8225-0020-5
Library of Congress Catalog Card Number: 75-7007

2   3   4   5   6   7   8   9   10   85   84   83   82   81   80   79   78

Contents

Introduction

   While doing volunteer work in Peru, South
America, I met a young man who had once been
lost in the Andes Mountains. For three days he was
alone, without food, shelter, or any means of
making a fire. The search party looking for him
expected to find him dead, just as they had often
found others who had become lost in those mountains. But that did not happen. The young man's
continual calls for help were heard by the searchers,
and he was rescued. He had survived his ordeal by
remaining calm and by using his energy in ways
helpful to himself. He alternately searched for food,
protected himself from the cold, and rested. The
young man told me that if it hadn't been for the
survival instruction he received as a child, he would
not have survived his three days in the mountains.

   The young man's story started me thinking about
the many times I had read of children and adults
who had died needlessly in emergency situations.
Either the victims had acted incorrectly in trying
to save themselves, or the rescuers had acted in-

correctly in trying to provide help. The young man's story also reminded me that emergency situations can occur at any time to anyone, regardless of age. Because emergencies usually occur quickly and without warning, a correct and rapid response may often mean the difference between life and death.

As a parent, teacher, and public speaker, I know that no one is too young to be taught correct reactions to common emergencies. Learning how to react in emergency situations should not be put off because you think that an adult *might* be present and *might* know what to do if an emergency were to occur. Nor should learning be put off by using the excuse that most people seldom find themselves in emergency situations.

The typical reaction of untrained people to an emergency is panic, shock, fear, and helplessness. But those who know how to react correctly to emergencies do not panic—they *respond*.

This book will alert you to some common emergencies that could happen to you during your lifetime. Through your reading, you will learn the correct responses to these specific emergencies.

And you will learn how to make good, clear-headed responses to any emergency you may encounter in the future.

KNOWING WHAT TO DO CAN PREVENT AN EMERGENCY FROM BECOMING A DIS-ASTER.

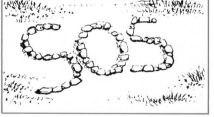

FIRE!

Should you be afraid of fire because it is hot and can burn or even kill you? Should you be afraid of fire because it has destroyed many homes and forest areas?

Fire has always been a good friend to human beings. A bright, warm fire has saved many lives by keeping people warm, cooking their food, and keeping dangerous animals away from them. Fire has also been used to light rooms and other dark places.

Fire will never harm you if you know how to use it correctly. Naturally you will burn your hand if you put it into a flame. But that is not using fire correctly. If you don't put your camp fire completely out, you may start a forest fire that could destroy many acres of trees. If you play with matches, you may very easily get burned or even set your house on fire. When fire is not used correctly, it can become your enemy instead of your friend. But as long as you know how to use fire and know how to respond to fire emergencies, you don't have to be afraid of fire.

Here are a few fire emergencies that could happen to you. Would you know what to do to keep the fire from harming you or others nearby?

Emergency 1 **Fire in your home**

You are at home watching television with your brothers and sisters. Your mother is in the kitchen cooking dinner. Suddenly you hear her yell "FIRE!"

WHAT SHOULD YOU DO?

If there is ever a fire in your house, the first thing to do is ESCAPE. Get outside where you are safe, and do not enter the house again. Once a fire gets out of control, only a trained fire fighter will be able to put it out. Don't waste time trying to put the fire out yourself, and don't waste time calling the fire department from inside your burning house. Many persons have been killed because they did not realize how fast fires flare up and spread. The heat from a small fire can cause an entire rug, curtain, or couch to burst into flames. That is why it is so important to get outside immediately. It is a good idea to have a *planned spot* outside the house where the whole family can meet in an emergency to make sure everyone is safe.

Once you are safely outside, you can call the fire department from a neighbor's phone. Dial the fire department directly if the phone number is available, or dial "0" and the operator will connect you with the local fire department. Be sure to give your NAME, ADDRESS, and TOWN. And be sure to report whether the fire is inside or outside the house. Don't hang up until you are sure your message has been understood. Many people are in such a hurry to report a fire that they forget to give the location of the fire. Then they wonder why it takes the fire department so long to get there!

A phone is the best way to contact the fire department, but you can use a fire box if no phone is available. Fire boxes are located on telephone poles on many street corners. Walk to the fire box nearest to your home, open the door of the fire box, and pull the alarm. When the alarm is set off, it will alert the fire department to a fire in your area. You should stay by the box until the fire

trucks come so that you can direct them to the fire.

Fire-alarm boxes are handy and have been used to save many lives. But when fire boxes are misused, great inconvenience and harm can be caused. A person who sends in a false alarm wastes the fire fighters' time and effort—time and effort that could have been used to put out another fire or to rescue a person trapped inside a burning building. It is illegal to send in a false alarm. A person accused of causing a false alarm runs the risk of being sent to jail or of being fined.

Emergency 2 **Fire breaks out during the night**

You are asleep at night in your bedroom. Suddenly you are awakened by the smell of smoke, and you think that you hear the crackling of a fire. But your bedroom door is closed, so you are not sure. Your parents are asleep in their room, and your brother is asleep in his room. Should you run out into the hall to check for a fire and to alert your family? Or should you stay in your room?

WHAT SHOULD YOU DO?

If there *is* a fire and you open your door to check, you could be killed instantly — even if the fire were downstairs. The heat from a fire on the first floor would quickly rise to the second floor. This heat could be as hot as 1,000 degrees, and it would scorch, or burn, your lungs the minute you opened your door. If the intense heat did not hurt you, the poisonous gas fumes of the fire would cause you to die of suffocation. The most important thing to remember is this:

NEVER OPEN YOUR DOOR IF YOU SUS-
PECT A FIRE, UNLESS YOU USE THE
DOOR TEST TO FIND OUT IF THERE *IS*
A FIRE.

The door test is quite simple to do. Place your hands on the door and doorknob to feel if they are warm. If either the door or the doorknob is the least bit warm—don't open the door. If you have some towels or rags, stuff them around the cracks of your door. This is important because there may be poisonous gases, hot air, and possibly even flames outside your door. You may shout to alert your family, but tell them not to open their doors either. If you live with sick or aged people who are unable to escape, tell them to stay in their rooms with their doors tightly sealed. Let them know that you will send help. Then, escape through your window to a nearby tree, roof, or garage top, and wait for help. If you can lower yourself to the ground with a ladder, a rope, or some bedsheets tied to your bed, do it. Drop to the ground from your window *only* if there is no other way to escape.

If your door was cool when you tested it, you can

open it. But be careful not to open it too quickly. Brace your shoulder and foot against the door and open it slowly, for if there is a fire, the force of the air and heat will push the door open. If the air is not too hot when you open the door, crawl on the floor to another room or exit. You should crawl in order to avoid the heat and poisonous gases in the air, which rise upward. Also put a wet cloth or handkerchief over your mouth and nose to prevent your lungs from being scorched when you breathe.

The members of your family should be able to escape outside by themselves. Once outside, you should all meet at the special meeting place in order to count noses. Be sure to contact the fire department right away.

Emergency 3 **Your clothes catch fire**

You are busy performing some experiments for your friends with your new chemistry set. You light your candle or bunsen burner, and the next thing you know, your clothes are on fire. The fire is all around you, and you cannot see or breathe well. Should you wait for your friends to help you? Should you yell and scream for help? Should you run outside? Should you try to put the fire out yourself?

WHAT SHOULD YOU DO?

Many children have died or have been seriously burned because they either screamed or ran for help instead of smothering the flames themselves. You must act immediately in this emergency, as in all emergencies. Either rip off your burning clothing and put out the fire, or just roll yourself up in a rug or blanket to smother the flames. You could also just roll on the ground until the fire is out. When the flames have no air, they will die out. If there is a shower near you, you could also jump in and turn on the water.

Emergency 4 **Fire in a public place**

You are in a crowded movie theater enjoying yourself. Suddenly someone yells "FIRE!" Immediately, people rush out of their seats and run to get out of the theater. Where should you go?

WHAT SHOULD YOU DO?

In any public area, the fire exits are clearly marked. If a fire breaks out in a public area, you should always head for the fire exit nearest you. Most people are killed in a fire because they try to get out the same way they entered. Death also results when people are in too big a *hurry* to get out. Many people are trampled to death by others hurrying over them. If you are in a public building when a fire breaks out, do not yell, scream, or even talk because then you may not hear some emergency instructions being given.

Emergency 5 A neighbor's house is on fire

You are walking down the street. You notice smoke coming from a neighbor's house. As you get nearer to the house, you realize it is on fire. Are there people in the house who need help? Do they know their house is on fire?

WHAT SHOULD YOU DO?

If you suspect a house is on fire, the first thing you should do is to ring the doorbell or pound on the door to alert any persons inside. Never enter the house, however, even if someone inside calls for help. You must quickly call the fire department from another house or use the fire-alarm box. When you call, be sure to give your name and address and, more important, the address of the house on fire.

Emergency 6 **Fire in the woods**

You and your friends are playing in a large wooded field. Your friend brings out a pack of matches. You begin to light the matches, and eventually a small fire starts. You are unable to put this fire out, and it grows rapidly because the day is windy and there is a lot of dry wood in the area. You know that fire fighters are needed to put the blaze out, for it is spreading quickly. The fire could even spread to nearby houses. But you are afraid to report the fire because you know that you have done wrong and will be punished.

WHAT SHOULD YOU DO?

Never play with fire or matches. Without meaning to, you may cause a large fire. A small burning match or twig is all that is needed to start a fire that can destroy an entire house, building, or even a forest. If you accidentally start a fire, first *escape from injury* and then *call the police or the fire department* immediately. The fire department's main concern will be to put out the fire. This is easier to do when the fire is small than when it is large and out of control.

Honesty is the best policy. It is far better to admit your action openly than to run away and be reported by others. You could be sent to the Juvenile Bureau for starting a fire and not reporting it.

LIGHTNING

Are you afraid of thunder and lightning? Do you try to hide from thunder whenever you hear it? Are you afraid that you will be struck and killed by a bolt of lightning?

Long ago, human beings were afraid of lightning and thunder because they did not know what these mysterious things were. They thought that lightning and thunder were signs that the gods were angry with them. It was only 200 years ago that people finally discovered what lightning and thunder really are. In 1708 a man named William Wall guessed that lightning was really electricity. Then, in 1752, Benjamin Franklin did his famous kite experiment in a lightning storm. He proved that a flash of lightning was really a huge and powerful bolt of electricity.

Lightning is an electric charge so strong and powerful that it actually lights up the sky as it travels through the atmosphere. Though a bolt of lightning lasts for only half a second, it produces enough electricity to light a 100-watt bulb for more than three months. Lightning is so hot that it heats up the air around it. When cooler air meets the air heated by lightning, thunder results. This is why you hear a loud clap of thunder after you see a bolt of lightning.

Lightning may travel from cloud to cloud, or it may travel from the sky to the ground. It always takes the quickest path to the ground by striking the tallest object in its path. It then travels through this object and enters the ground. The tallest object may be a building, a tree, a house, a fence, or even a person.

Once you understand what lightning really is, and once you know how to avoid being in its path, you won't have to be afraid of it. Let's see if you know what to do in the following emergencies.

Emergency 1 **Caught outdoors in a thunderstorm**

You and your family are enjoying a picnic on a sunny summer's day. You have just finished eating your picnic lunch, and you have decided to play a game of baseball with your friends in an open field.

While you are playing, the sky suddenly becomes dark, and it begins to rain. You see a flash of lightning, and you hear a loud crash of thunder. Because you are getting soaked, you want to take cover. But your family car is parked in a lot that is very far from the picnic area. As you try to decide what to do, you notice that there is a large tree nearby. Its branches are long and full of leaves—a perfect shelter from the storm. Should you run to the tree?

WHAT SHOULD YOU DO?

Lightning storms develop quickly. Without much warning, they can ruin your summer outings or even cause a death. If you are caught in a lightning storm, don't run under a tree to keep dry even though you are getting soaked. Lightning always strikes the tallest object in its path—and in this case the tree would be the tallest object.

A nearby building or your car would be the safest place to go during a lightning storm. A building has a steel frame surrounding it. Lightning will pass through this metal and go into the ground where it becomes harmless. If you are in a car or a building during a storm, be sure not to touch anything metal or you may be seriously burned.

If there are no buildings or cars near you, make sure that *you* are not the tallest object in the area. Find a ditch or ravine, or just duck down and remain low until the storm passes. As long as you are not the tallest object, you will be safe.

Emergency 2 Swimming during a thunderstorm

You are with your friends, swimming in a lake. The sun is slowly being covered by dark clouds. You hear some thunder, but it seems to be far away. You even think you see a small flash of lightning in the distance. Because it hasn't started to rain yet, and because you are having such a good time, you decide to stay in the water.

As you continue playing in the water, the lightning seems to be getting nearer, and the thunder seems to be getting louder and louder. But it is still not raining.

WHAT SHOULD YOU DO?

Lightning storms not only develop quickly, but they also occur without much of a warning—and sometimes without any rain. The minute you see the sky darken, you should be on the alert for a storm. As soon as you hear thunder or see lightning, no matter how far away it seems, you should head for land as quickly as possible.

You need not fear a lightning storm as long as

you protect yourself from it. The quicker you get to shore, the safer you will be, because water is a great conductor, or carrier, of electricity. A person in a lake that is hit by lightning may be killed instantly.

No matter how much fun you may be having, don't take a chance when your life is involved. It is better to ruin your fun than to take a swim that may be your last.

Emergency 3 **At home during a thunderstorm**

You are inside your house watching television in your living room. Your sister is listening to the radio, and your mother is in the kitchen washing the supper dishes.

The telephone rings, and you answer it. While you are talking on the phone, a thunderstorm begins.

WHAT SHOULD YOU DO?

Many people think they are safe in a thunderstorm as long as they are in their homes. But many people have been burned by lightning right inside their homes because they did not know what safety measures to take during a storm. Remember that lightning will strike the tallest object. The tallest object may not be your house, but it could be your television aerial or even the telephone pole outside your house.

During an electric storm, you should immediately hang up the telephone, because phones act as conductors of electricity. Many people will hear the static, or electric disturbance, as they talk, but they will still continue talking. If lightning happens to strike the telephone line you are using, the loud noise could damage your hearing. And you could be badly burned by the heat of the electrical charge as it actually melts the phone in your hand!

The television set and the radio should also be turned off. Your mother should stop doing the dishes and be sure not to touch the metal faucets. They, too, may be conductors of electricity. Stay away from any open or closed windows or any doorways. Just wait patiently until the storm passes. And don't worry—you are probably safe from danger.

EMERGENCIES IN THE WATER

Water is a source of life to all people—without water we would surely die. Three-quarters of our earth is covered with water. Two-thirds of our bodies are made of water. Each day we need water to drink, to wash ourselves, and to prepare our foods. Water is a source of the animal and plant life that we eat.

Humans have always known the importance of water to life. Every primitive society lived near a source of water. When people found out that objects could float on water, water became a means for travel. People made dugout canoes, rafts, boats, and eventually large ships. And when people realized that water could also supply electric power, they made water wheels to generate electricity.

Water has also been used for recreation. Swimming, water skiing, boating, fishing, diving, ice skating and other ice sports have provided human beings with many hours of fun and healthy recreation. Most people have pleasant memories of their swimming outings at a lake or their vacations on an ocean beach.

Unfortunately, water has also been the cause of death for many people. The people who died either acted foolishly in water, or they became frightened of it and allowed their fears to rule them. Every person and animal with lungs can float on water. So even nonswimmers would never drown if they stayed calm and knew what to do in an emergency. Here are some water emergencies that could happen to you. Would you know how to act? Most of these situations were written especially for non-swimmers, but they could happen to swimmers too.

Emergency 1 Rescuing a drowning friend

You and your friend are playing near a water hole. Your friend slips and falls into the water. He cannot swim and neither can you. He is drowning, and he calls for your help. No one else is around, and you would not have enough time to run for help. Even though you cannot swim, you wonder if you should jump in and try to save him.

WHAT SHOULD YOU DO?

The most foolish thing you could do would be to jump in and try to save your friend. Unless you are a skilled swimmer and a trained life saver, you would be of no help to him. You would probably *both* drown. Even a trained lifeguard jumps in only as a last resort. Lifeguards usually row out to drowning victims and tow them to shore.

Since no one is around to help you, you must act fast. Try to calm your friend by telling him to tread water while you try to give him something to grab onto. If he is near enough to you, you could stretch your arm out to him and pull him in. If he is farther out, you could use a stick or a pole, or even throw your belt, shirt, or trousers to reach him and pull him in. Before you pull the victim to shore, lie down and make sure you are well anchored. Otherwise, you could be pulled into the water with him.

If your friend cannot be reached at all, try to find an object that will float, and throw it to him. A life preserver, a big ball, a raft, a plastic picnic cooler, or even a thermos will do. Tell him to put

this floating object under his chin and to float to
shore on it.

Emergency 2 Rescuing yourself from drowning

Even though you don't know how to swim, you decide to go fishing. All of your friends are busy, so you go alone. The water looks cool and shallow, and you are so hot. You decide to take your shoes and socks off and stand in the water to keep cool. As you step into the water, you slip on a rock and discover that what at first looked like a pool of shallow water is really a very deep hole.

You sink underwater and try to come up again. You are scared, so your body becomes stiff. You begin to claw and struggle to get to the surface. You come to the top, but you breathe in some water. This makes you cough and choke. Now, with no air in your lungs, you sink again. You are becoming very tired, but you try to reach the surface and stay afloat. No one is around to help you.

WHAT SHOULD YOU DO?

First of all, you should always have someone with you when you swim or when you are even *near* water. (This is called the buddy system.) Next, you should know that the human body is a life preserver when the lungs are filled with air. If you remain calm, it is almost impossible to drown, even if you can't swim. But if you panic, stiffen up, and wildly wave your arms and legs, you will tire yourself out. Then you will either faint, or you will swallow water and sink.

If you remain calm, you can stay afloat for many hours until help comes. Nonswimmers have been known to stay afloat for as long as 12 hours by *treading water.* Treading water is a simple method of keeping your head above water. Here are the steps:

1. Open and close your legs like a scissor, keeping up a steady rhythm.

2. At the same time, keep your arms in motion in front of you. With your elbows slightly bent, move your hands away from each other—palms out—and bring them together again—palms facing. Keep your hands and forearms moving back and forth like this in a steady rhythm.

3. Now, with your head above water, you will

be able to inhale through your mouth, thus inflating your lungs to act as life preservers.

4. In a steady, relaxed manner, continue your treading movements.

Emergency 3 Your boat overturns

You are in a rowboat on a lake. Someone in the boat stands and tips the boat over. You and the rest of the crew are thrown into the water as the boat overturns.

WHAT SHOULD YOU DO?

"Stick with the ship" is the best thing for you to remember. Use the overturned boat to keep yourself afloat. Never desert the boat unless you are near enough to shore to swim in, or unless you are headed for a waterfall or rapids.

If only two of you are in the water, join hands over the bottom of the overturned boat and rest on the boat as you both float. A small craft, like a canoe, is light enough to float even when it is filled with water. Always be prepared for a possible boating emergency by wearing a life jacket.

Emergency 4 Escaping from a sinking car

You and your family are driving over country roads. As you cross an old bridge, your car skids off the edge and plunges into the river below.

Your car begins to sink. The car windows are closed, but as the car sinks deeper and deeper, water begins to seep in. You try to open the doors to get out, but the doors won't open because of the great water pressure around the car. Your family is trapped in the car as it slowly goes down.

WHAT SHOULD YOU DO?

If you have fast enough reflexes, you could immediately open the door before the car begins to sink. Most likely, however, you will not have enough time to open the door because the car will sink quickly upon entering the water. The best thing for you to do is to remain calm while the car sinks. There will be enough air in the car to enable you to breathe and make your escape plans.

You will be unable to escape through the doors

because of the great water pressure around your car. The windows will be the only way to escape. Roll the windows partly down to let the water fill your car as it sinks. You can escape through the windows only when your car is nearly full of water. But the more water that fills the car, the less air you will have to breathe. So you must act quickly. Inhale deeply through your mouth, hold your breath, and escape by swimming through the nearest open window. With your lungs full of air, you will float to the surface. Once you have reached the surface, you will be safe. You can either swim to shore, or tread water to stay afloat until you are rescued.

Remember not to panic when your car is filling with water and the doors won't open. Stay calm, and you will escape.

Emergency 5 How to give artificial respiration

Your friend was drowning, and you have just pulled her out of the water. She has been under water for a few minutes and is unconscious. You think she might be dead, but you are not sure.

WHAT SHOULD YOU DO?

Begin artificial respiration immediately. A few seconds may mean the difference between life and death. The longer a person is submerged in water, the less chance he or she will have of being revived. But a person who has been under water not more than five minutes can usually be revived by artificial respiration.

Here is the proper way to give artificial respiration:

1. Make sure the person is lying face upward. Then, using your finger, *clear the mouth of foreign objects.*

2. Tilt the head back with the chin up. Pull the jaw upward so that it juts out. Keep the victim's head in this position so that the passage to the lungs remains open.

3. Open your mouth and place it *tightly* over the victim's mouth. Pinch the nostrils closed to keep the air from escaping. (A second method you could use is to put your mouth over the person's nose and close the mouth.)

4. Breathe into the person's mouth until the chest
rises. Count to four and take another deep breath.
Blow into the victim's mouth again. Keep repeating
this process.

Don't give up. Continue to give artificial respiration until help comes. The person may be revived in
a few tries, or you may have to continue for more
than an hour. But don't stop trying until the person
is either revived or pronounced legally dead by
a physician.

TIPS FOR WATER SAFETY

1. The best prevention for drowning is to learn how to swim. The better a swimmer you are, the less chance you have of drowning. Three out of four persons who drown are non-swimmers.

2. Where can you learn how to swim? Although many persons learn how to swim from their parents and friends, there are many courses given by swimming instructors at youth clubs, community centers, and summer camps.

3. Because the body is its own natural life preserver, even nonswimmers will not drown if they remain calm and let their bodies float naturally. In an emergency, all a nonswimmer must do is take in air when the body needs it and wait until help comes.

4. Whether you are a swimmer or a nonswimmer, you should always be with a buddy in a supervised swimming area. Half of all drownings

usually occur in unguarded areas where persons are swimming alone. Very few drownings occur when a lifeguard is present.

5. If you ever get a cramp while you are swimming, don't panic, even if you are in deep water. A cramp will not harm you if you remain calm and know what to do for it. Massage the cramped area, whether it is a leg or an arm. Rubbing will force the tightened muscle to relax. Then the cramp will go away. To avoid getting cramps, don't swim immediately after eating or if you are too tired.

DANGER! THIN ICE

When winter comes and the temperature drops below the freezing point—32 degrees Fahrenheit—ice begins to form on ponds, lakes, rivers, and streams. These slippery surfaces can provide hours of fun for children and adults who like to ice skate or ride ice boats.

Fun on the ice can suddenly become tragedy, however, if people venture onto thin ice. The ice on a pond or lake forms first along the water's edge. Here, the water is not too deep, so it freezes quickly and solidly. Toward the center of the pond, the water is deeper and may be warmer than 32 degrees. The center is the last part of the pond to freeze, and it does not freeze as solidly as the water along the banks. So what looks like a thick, solid ice surface in the center of the pond may really be a *thin* ice covering.

Before you select a pond, lake, or river to skate on, make sure it is safe. The ice's depth should be measured and declared thick enough to support you as well as other skaters. Also, remember that ice changes as the temperature changes. After a warm spell, ice will melt, becoming thinner and more dangerous to skate on.

Let us look at a few emergency situations that could happen to you on ice. What would you do in each of these situations?

Emergency 1 **A friend falls through thin ice**

It is a cold winter day. You and your friend decide to go ice skating on a frozen pond in the woods. The ice looks solid and safe. While you are still putting on your skates, your friend rushes onto the ice and begins skating. All of a sudden, you see him fall through the ice and plunge into the icy water. He calls for your help and grabs for the ice around him, but it breaks. Should you skate over to him to pull him out?

WHAT SHOULD YOU DO?

You will have to act quickly to help your friend, for a person can survive only about 15 to 30 min-

utes in freezing water without becoming frozen. But if you rush over to the hole, you would be of no help to your friend because you would probably plunge through the ice too.

The first thing you should do is to find a long pole, a hockey stick, rope, ladder, or even a sled that you can extend to your friend to pull him out. Then lie down on the ice and crawl very carefully to the hole. Crawling will keep you from crashing through the ice because in that position your weight is spread over a large area. Once you are near enough to the victim, you can extend something to him and pull him out.

If other children are on the ice they, too, can help. By lying down in a column and holding onto the ankles of the person in front of them, the group can form a human chain across the ice. The whole chain can crawl to the hole, and the first person can grab the hands of the person in the water.

Then the whole chain can slowly move backwards and pull the victim out of the water.

Once your friend is out of the water, tell him not to stand up on the ice or he may fall through again. On thin ice, always *crawl* to safety.

Emergency 2 **You fall through thin ice**

You are skating alone and there is no one else around. You hear a crack. The next thing you know, you have crashed through the ice and are surrounded by freezing water. You grab for the ice around you, but each time you grab to pull yourself out, the ice breaks. You feel yourself getting cold and numb. You are tired and exhausted. You sink under the cold water and come up again. You scream for help, but no one hears you.

WHAT SHOULD YOU DO?

Because the ice is too weak to hold your body weight, you will have to break a path through the thin ice to reach a more solid area. To do this, hold onto the edge of the ice with one hand for support. Use the other hand to break a path through the ice. One man is known to have saved himself by breaking a 100-foot path through the ice until he reached solid ground.

Before *you* reach solid ground, you may reach a more solid area of ice. If you do, kick and squirm to boost yourself out of the water and up onto the ice. When you succeed, you can crawl away until you reach solid ground.

SOME DO'S AND DON'TS ON THE ICE

1. The ice you skate on should be at least two to four inches thick, preferably thicker. *Don't skate until it is declared safe by your local fire department.*

2. Always skate with a friend. Besides having more fun skating with friends, you would have help if an emergency were to occur.

3. Never build a fire on the ice to keep warm. This only weakens the ice around you.

4. Try not to gather in large groups in one spot on the ice.

5. Always be careful when you skate. The blades of ice skates can cause accidents. Be alert to avoid collisions or dangerous falls. Watch out for others who fall so that you can avoid hitting them.

6. It is best to skate in a large public area that you know is safe for skating.

ANIMALS AND INSECTS

Animals and insects are very interesting creatures to watch and learn from. Yet, many people are afraid of them. Perhaps when they were children, these people were frightened by a barking dog, an insect that buzzed near them, or a harmless snake that suddenly crawled from under a log they were playing on. Because they never got over their fear, they think that all animals and insects are harmful. Of course, this isn't true.

Most animals and insects are helpful to humans. As we know, many animals are kept as pets. Some animals supply us with the medicine we need. Deadly snake venom, for instance, is only one of the animal products used to make medicine. Animal furs and skins clothe and protect us. Animals and insects are also used for food. Some, like cows and bees, actually *produce* food for us. Other animals help crops grow by killing insects that destroy crops.

Animals and insects can hurt us too, of course. The bee that makes honey can also sting us. And the termite that helps to enrich soil by aiding the decay of wood can also destroy our homes. Some insects destroy crops, while other insects carry disease. A dog that is one person's loving pet can become frightened of strangers and attack them.

It is important to remember that most animals are not out to hurt us. Many animals that attack us do so only because they are afraid that we may be trying to hurt them. Instead of being afraid of all animals and insects because a few might harm us, we should learn which ones are really harmful. Then we should learn what to do if we ever come in contact with any of them.

Here are some emergency situations involving harmful animals and insects. If any of these things happened to you, what would you do?

Emergency 1 **A dog attacks you**

You are walking down the street. As you walk past a yard with an open gate, a big, snarling, unfriendly dog runs out. The animal stops near you and begins to growl—it looks as though it is ready

to attack you. You do not see the dog's owner.
Should you run away? Should you scream for help?

WHAT SHOULD YOU DO?

If you were to run from a dog that is unfriendly,
it might attack you. This is because animals become
excited when they see a moving object. If you were
to scream and act frightened, you would frighten
the dog and make it want to attack you.

The best thing to do is to stand still and act calm

so that the dog doesn't get excited. Stand with your legs together and your arms folded on your chest. When you are in this position, there is little of your body that the dog can grab onto. Talk very firmly and calmly to the dog to show it that you are not afraid—even though you are.

The dog may calm down when it sees you standing perfectly still and talking softly. When you see the dog calm down, you may try to take one step backward, moving away from it. If the dog does not object, take another step. Keep taking steps until you can walk away slowly. But remain facing the dog each time you take a step backward.

If the dog *does* attack you and starts to bite you, try to climb the nearest and highest object you can find. Climbing a tree, a fence, or even the nearest car will prevent the dog from harming you anymore.

If the dog crouches and attempts to leap at you, use your folded arms to throw the dog off balance while it is in the air. If you are knocked down by the dog, and it begins to attack you while you are on the ground, fold your arms over your face and try to lie perfectly still. Don't try to fight a dog when you are on the ground, unless the dog is so small that you will be able to get up quickly. If you lie perfectly still and don't move, the dog may lose interest and walk away. This is because dogs generally do not attack nonmoving objects.

Emergency 2 What to do for animal bites

You and your friend are pretending to be fighting. Your friend's pet dog thinks its master is in danger, so it bites you.

WHAT SHOULD YOU DO?

Whether you are bitten by a pet dog, cat, hamster, or even a wild squirrel or skunk, you must act quickly. A seemingly harmless bite may contain the germs of many diseases, especially rabies. Rabies is an animal disease that could prove deadly to you.

The most important thing for you to do after being bitten is to seek adult help in capturing the animal. It is best to call the police for this. Once the animal is captured, it can be tested for diseases. If the animal is not captured, the person who was bitten may have to undergo a series of shots to prevent rabies.

After getting help from an adult, treat the wound by washing it very carefully with soap and water. Make sure you wipe all the animal's saliva away. Once you have washed and cleaned the wound and the bleeding has stopped, cover the wound with a gauze dressing. Then get medical attention right away.

Emergency 3 **Snakes**

You and your friends are camping out for the weekend in a forest area. You have decided to go into the woods for a nature hike. As you walk over rocks, grass, and sticks, you come across a dead log in your path. Without thinking, you kick the log out of your way. Underneath the log is a snake that you have awakened and surprised. Should you scream and run away?

WHAT SHOULD YOU DO?

Whenever you hike in the woods, you should always be very careful where you step, for you may disturb a snake or other animal. Tall grass, decayed logs and trees, or openings in the ground and on hillsides may be the homes of many animals.

You should try to wear high leather boots whenever you go hiking, since three out of four snake bites are usually made in the legs. Leather boots, heavy slacks, or leather leggings offer you the best protection from snake bite.

Most snakes, even the most poisonous ones, are really afraid of people. A snake will usually bite you if it thinks it is in danger. If you stay perfectly still, a frightened snake will probably not attack you. But if you become scared, scream, or move quickly, the snake will bite you.

Slowly and calmly, take small steps backwards until you are a safe distance from the snake. It will be unable to strike at you from a distance of four to five feet or more. A surprising fact is that a snake is really a very slow animal. A person walking can easily outdistance the fastest moving snake. Once you are out of the snake's striking distance, you can either walk away or run away.

Emergency 4 **What to do for snake bites**

You are walking through the woods with your friends, collecting rocks, leaves, and insect specimens. Your friend stoops down to pick up an interesting rock. All of a sudden, she is bitten on the arm by a snake.

WHAT SHOULD YOU DO?

The most important thing to remember is that most snakes are nonpoisonous. Snake bites rarely ever result in death if there is immediate and proper first aid. But some persons—especially children—become so frightened when they are bitten by a snake that they actually die from fright or shock. They probably remember seeing stories of deadly snakes on television, and they think all snakes are poisonous.

All you have to do in treating an ordinary snake bite is to wash the wound carefully and then cover it. The wound will give you very little pain, and it will not swell very much.

Even though most snakes are nonpoisonous, you should know about the four types of poisonous snakes in North America. The four poisonous snakes are the rattlesnake, copperhead, coral, and cottonmouth, or water moccasin. These snakes are found mainly in the south and southwestern

United States. But the rattlesnake and copperhead can be found in some northern areas. (Look at the picture on the next page to make sure you are familiar with the way these snakes look.)

If you are bitten by one of these poisonous snakes, you will know it, even if you do not recognize what kind of snake bit you. You will have much pain and swelling, and you will feel weak, dizzy, or even sick to your stomach.

The most important thing to do for anyone bitten by a poisonous snake is to keep the person quiet and to get a doctor. If the victim gets medical attention within an hour of being bitten, he or she should be safe. While waiting for the doctor, a handkerchief or some other piece of cloth may be tied above the wound to stop the bleeding. Be sure it is not tied too tightly. The cloth should be loosened for 1 minute every 10 minutes so that blood can flow normally through the arm. Besides the piece of cloth, a cold pack may also be used to slow the bleeding.

If you cannot reach a doctor within an hour's time, or if the bite is a severe one on the person's neck or face, have a trained person use a snake-bite kit. You should always carry a snake-bite kit

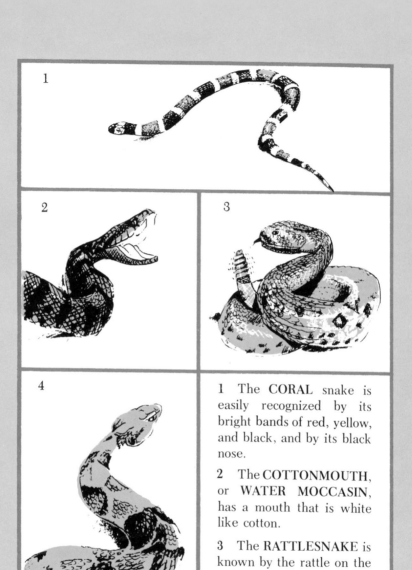

1 The **CORAL** snake is easily recognized by its bright bands of red, yellow, and black, and by its black nose.

2 The **COTTONMOUTH**, or **WATER MOCCASIN**, has a mouth that is white like cotton.

3 The **RATTLESNAKE** is known by the rattle on the end of its tail.

4 The **COPPERHEAD** snake is a copper or reddish-brown color.

59

when you are in areas known to have poisonous snakes. The kit should only be used when proper medical care is not available to treat a poisonous snake bite.

Emergency 5 **What to do for insect bites**

You are playing with your friends when a bee stings you. It hurts for a moment, but it doesn't seem very important so you continue playing. You have been stung by a bee before, and you remember that it was nothing serious. But now, as you play, you start to feel tired and ill. You have cramps and you feel sick to your stomach. Your skin becomes quite red and irritated.

WHAT SHOULD YOU DO?

One of every two people who die from bites of poisonous animals die from bee and wasp stings. If a snake or a scorpion bit you, you would be quite concerned about it, wouldn't you? Yet, most people don't think there is anything to worry about if they are stung by a wasp or a bee.

If you are stung by a bee for the *first time*, you really don't have to worry about it, for a first sting is rarely ever deadly. Normally there is slight pain, swelling, and redness where the sting occurred. Just wash and clean the area with soap and water. Then put a cold pack on it and perhaps some calamine lotion if it itches.

If you are stung a *second time* by a wasp or a bee, you must be very careful to notice whether or not you have stronger reactions to the sting. Some people may become very ill with a second bee sting. If you have any of the symptoms of the person in our story—very red and irritated skin, cramps, dizziness, and nausea—you had better see a doctor right away, for this second sting could be deadly. Your doctor will know how to help you so that you will not die from the sting. The doctor may give you a series of shots that will enable your body to survive other bee stings you might get. Your doctor may also give you a special kit to use if you are ever stung again.

As long as you do not ignore the distress signals your body gives you, you will never have to worry about a bee or wasp sting. Rarely has anyone ever died from a sting without first having many warnings. The people who did die ignored the warnings their bodies gave them and did not see a doctor.

HELP!
I'M LOST

Almost all of us, at one time or another, have found ourselves alone in an unfamiliar place. Perhaps we were in a store with our parents and turned around to find them gone. We may have been in a new school and could not find our room, in a theater and forgot where our seat was, or in a parking lot and forgot where our car was parked.

There is no reason to get scared and panic when we become lost. If we remain calm, we can think things out and decide upon the wisest thing to do. Usually, there are people around who will help us. Or there are telephones we can use to call home or to call a friend for help.

At times, help is not so easily available. Many of us have heard stories of persons who were stranded in a snowstorm or who became lost in a forest or a desert, or on a mountain. Many of these people were able to survive for days and weeks until they were rescued. Many others found their way to safety. But some did not survive. Perhaps they did not remain calm enough to think of ways to help themselves.

Imagine the many places *you* could be lost. Then read the following emergency situations. If you were lost in these places, what would you do?

Emergency 1 Lost in the woods

You are hiking in the woods with a few of your friends. You are so interested in all you see that you don't notice you have become separated from your friends. You aren't too worried, though, for you are sure you'll find them soon. You continue walking for another 15 minutes. But you still do not find your friends. You call for them, but you hear no answer. You decide to turn back, but you have forgotten the way you came. You are starting to get a little worried now, so you keep calling as you walk. The sun is going down, and it seems that you are walking in circles. When you finally realize that you are lost, you begin to worry. It will soon be dark, and your friends are nowhere in sight.

WHAT SHOULD YOU DO?

Whenever you hike, you should carry some type
of emergency kit. In this kit you should have
matches to start a fire, a compass to tell your direction, a knife, some candy bars, a string and some
hooks for fishing, and a few first aid materials.
This kit would be very important to you if you ever
became lost in the woods.

The most important thing to do whenever you
are lost is to stay calm. Screaming, crying, or just
running in any direction will not help you. In fact,
doing these things will only get you more upset.
If you run, you may travel even deeper into the
woods. So stop where you are and try to get your
location straight. It is better to stay in one spot
while you wait for help than it is to wander in one
direction hoping to find your way.

If you are not found by the time night falls,
don't panic. Find an open area or a high place
where you can be seen if help comes for you. Then
build a fire. The fire will keep you warm, keep
animals away, and perhaps help rescuers find you.
Gather some dry twigs, pine needles, and wood

shavings. These things will be the tinder for your
fire. If you don't have a match to light your fire,
find a pointed twig and rub it on a stone. The fric-
tion from this rubbing will cause sparks that will
set fire to the tinder. Once the tinder is lit, the
flames will spread to the twigs you have placed
around the tinder. If the ground is too wet to start
a fire, use some rocks or logs on which to place
your tinder.

Once you have started one fire to keep warm,

you can build another to serve as an *S.O.S.* signal. In the daytime you can send smoke signals by adding wet green leaves to the fire. You can also use rocks to spell out the letters *S.O.S.* in a clearing. Perhaps someone on a hike or someone in a search plane would see it. Also, if you have a mirror, catch the sun's reflection in it and flash it back and forth. This flashing light can be seen for miles.

Call out for help every 5 to 10 minutes. It is far better for you to call for help from one location than to walk around aimlessly getting tired and exhausted. As long as you remain calm and don't worry, help will come to you and you will be safe.

Though it is best to stay in one spot while you wait for help, there are sometimes good reasons for starting out to *find* help. If you have not been rescued after a day or two, or if your food supply is running out, you should try to find your way to a settlement. If you can, climb a nearby tree or hill and look for a campsite, a road, a river, or a town in the distance. If you see any of these things, get your direction set before you start traveling toward it. Use your compass to direct you. If you have no compass, plot a course in a straight line. You can do this by lining up three landmarks visually as you walk—one directly behind you, one where you are, and one directly ahead of you. Perhaps you can line up three trees. If you remember to do this, you will always be walking in a straight line.

Wherever you walk, make sure you leave a marked trail in case you want to backtrack. A marked trail will also help your friends find you much faster. To mark a trail, attach torn bits of clothing to branches, make a pile of stones every few feet, or shape arrows from twigs or stones to point your direction. Be careful not to tear bark off the trees or break branches, however, for this is destructive to nature.

Emergency 2 **Lost in a public place**

It is not likely that you will get lost in the woods often in your life. It is, however, very easy for you to become separated from your parents or friends in a big store, in a large parking lot, in a stadium, in a movie theater, at the beach, or on the street of a big city. Would you know what to do if you were separated from your parents or friends in any of these places?

WHAT SHOULD YOU DO?

Any time you go some place with your family or friends, it is a good idea to select a spot where you can all meet in case one person gets separated from the others. This spot can be the place where your car is parked, or it can be the main entrance to a building. Make sure that you all know where the meeting spot is.

If you have not selected a special meeting place, you will have to use common sense if you become separated from the others. The best thing for you to do is to stay calm. If you stay in one spot, or in the last spot you remember being with the others, you will be found. Staying in one spot is far better than running around in the crowds calling for help.

If a long period of time passes and you are still not found, you can always look for help. If you are at a beach, you can find a lifeguard to help you. If you are at a stadium, an attendant will help you. If you are in a big store or at any big gathering, there will be a main desk or a central area you can go to for help. If you are lost on the street, a policeman will be glad to help you.

Conclusion

The purpose of this book has been to make you aware of some common emergency situations and to show you how to handle them if you ever have to. Most important of all, the book has tried to help you develop a general attitude in response to *any* emergency. This attitude should be one of thinking and acting *on your own,* for you cannot always count on someone else to be around when an emergency occurs.

THINK AHEAD TO BE PREPARED FOR EMERGENCIES

Plan ahead before you take that camping or boating trip, go swimming, hiking, or ice skating, or take a long drive. Try to imagine emergencies that could arise in each situation. Then try to decide what you would do and what equipment you would need in order to help yourself. Thinking ahead will prepare you for action if an emergency should occur.

THINK AND RESPOND TO EMERGENCIES

If an emergency happens to you, *do not panic.* If your emergency is similar to one that you have read about in this book or in another book, try to recall what you should do and then do it. If your emergency is an unfamiliar one, you should try to work out the best possible response. In order to do that, always think carefully before you act. People who immediately panic will not act correctly. But those who remain calm enough to *think,* in spite of their fear, will save time and energy and will be able to act effectively.

Index

ABOUT THE AUTHOR

A teacher, lecturer, and innovator in the field of childhood education, Mary Lou Vandenburg is a person dedicated to enriching the learning experiences of children. After receiving a B.A. in elementary education from William Paterson College in New Jersey, Mrs. Vandenburg taught fourth grade in the New Jersey public school system. She has also done private tutoring through the schools and has worked with the Passaic (N.J.) Children's Bureau in giving individualized instruction to students at home. In 1968, Mrs. Vandenburg created the Parent Education Lecture Series, a program of lectures, seminars, and parent-teacher workshops on child development. Three years later, she initiated the Children's Program Series, a program of classroom and auditorium presentations dealing with topics not usually part of school curricula. This book is an outgrowth of one of those presentations.

Outside of her professional duties, Mrs. Vandenburg is a volunteer worker, active in children's service organizations such as hospitals and summer camps. Among her other interests are gardening, hiking, and traveling. She has also achieved a high level of competence in the sport of karate—she holds a brown belt. Mrs. Vandenburg lives in Clifton, New Jersey, with her husband and son.